MW00678785

4 HUSBANDS

3 DIVORCES

2 LOVERS

1 GOD

MY LIFE STORY

KIM V. MAYS

4 Husbands,3 Divorces, 2 Lovers,1 God : My Life Story

Copyright © 2018 Kim V. Mays

All rights reserved. This book or any portion thereof may not be reproduced or used in any manner whatsoever without the express written permission of the publisher except for the use of brief quotations in a book review. Printed in the United States of America

First Printing

978-1-943284-34-4 (pbk)
978-1-943284-36-8 (ebk)

A2Z Books, LLC
Lithonia, GA 30058
www.A2ZBooksPublishing.net
Manufactured in the United States of America A2Z Books Publishing has allowed this work to remain exactly as the author intended, verbatim.

In Loving Memory of
Stanley Brown, Jr. and Catherine Mays-Brown
Ben Mays Sr. and Bernell Mays
Ernest Walker
Abram Walker

Dedicated to
Glenn Sims and Family
Donesha Wells and Family
Sanaa Griffin
Mays Family

TABLE OF CONTENTS

FORWARD

This book will tell you the story of my life. How I was married four times, divorced three times, fell in love twice and through it all still have one God who saved me! I came up with the titles for the book chapters through my feelings for each individual and the characters that they portrayed. I also want to give credit to my oldest daughter who helped and inspired me with this book. I dedicate this book to my family, loved ones, and friends.

Introduction

I was born in a small town called Roosevelt, New York on August 10, 1965.

Long Island was a peaceful place, and this is where I grew up. My parents were Catherine Mays-Brown and Bruce Anthony Coles. I remember when my mother and father were dating, my father was not always around (Red Flag). I used to hear them arguing because my father could not stay overnight. Now I understand why; he was married. He was married with children and did not have any respect for his first wife. Back in those days, cheating was like an epidemic, and everyone was doing it! My parents dated for several months and my father divorced his first wife and married my mother.

My father's mother, who was my grandmother always made me feel like I was an illegitimate child but she loved me. She was an only child, and so was my father. She had been married four times just like me, but her last husband died during 911. I remember her being very stern and none of the other grandchildren liked her. Still, she was my grandmother; she passed in 2015. She outlived my mother who passed in 2010 and my father who died in 2009. My father did not have a good relationship with his mother, and I believe this was how the vicious cycle started.

My parents got married in Virginia in a little town called Pamplin. Before my parents got married, they had a house built. This was the first time I had ever seen a house built from scratch. I was about 11 years old, but I was too tall and mature for my age. People thought I was much older than I was. We lived in Virginia for almost two years before my mother left my father and moved to New York. She chose New York because she had a sister there.

I remember begging my mother to leave my father before something terrible happened (Red Flag). He was mentally and physically abusive to her and me. My mother was terrified of my father, and so was I. One day, I got into a fight on the school bus and got off the bus limping and crying. My Dad saw me, and he broke. He told me I had to be tough, fight back and don't let anyone run over me. He was a bully, and the neighbors even thought so.

One time I was lazy, I didn't want to get up and turn off the TV, so I did it with my foot and in the process, the knob fell off. When my father came home later in the day, he turned on the TV but discovered that the knob had fallen off. He started screaming at me, and I ran away. I ran to my aunt's house and hid behind her. He went outside and grabbed a sticker bush. I believe if it weren't for my aunt, he would have hurt me in a worse way. He just kept saying "your mother is going to pay for this TV." My mother finally got enough courage to leave him, so we moved to New York with my aunt, her kids, and my two uncles.

My parents separated, and my father moved in with another woman. My father had many kids by different women, and he abused every last one of them. I guess you could say "Papa was a Rolling Stone"! My mother was determined to take care of me and help the family. She worked 3-11 for more than 30 years at a hospital that in my opinion did not appreciate her. I had a lot of free time on my hands, and I used to do sneaky things. I did a lot of things I wish I could take back like stealing my bank book and withdrawing all of the money out of the account.

My mother did not find out for months, but I felt so bad about it.

My mother was Methodist, and my aunt was Pentecostal. My mother went to church almost every Sunday, and on several occasions, I went to church with her, but was I "saved?" No, but I did believe in God. I would also attend my aunt's church from time to time. I got baptized at my aunt's church, but I was not ready to change.

I started dating early, and I had my first boyfriend at the age of 14, his name was "Sonny B." Back in those days, we had nicknames with letters after them. Sonny used to suck his thumb which I thought was odd for a young man his age but he had a lot of family, and he knew how to fight. His family was well known in the neighborhood. I remember when he got into an argument with a guy at the local store and when the guy heard his name and realized who he was, he started running. No one in the neighborhood would "blank" with him.

I started high school that year, but I was not focused. I wanted to hang out with my friends and run the streets. My nickname in high school back in 1981 was "Special K." I named myself that after a famous rap group called "Treacherous Three"! The highlight of the neighborhood was going to the local skate rink. I went to the skating rink and saw the group called "Treacherous Three" in concert. I remember being up in the front and being able to reach out and touch them. That was a thrill for me.

My first boyfriend broke my heart. We dated for about a year, and he decided he wanted to be with someone else. He had already been seeing another girl, and I could feel something was going on. He stopped by to see me and we were in the basement talking. He said it was over. I cried my eyes out and tried to get him to change his mind but that did not work. Yes, I was hurt but eventually, I moved on. I was about to turn 15 and I wanted to celebrate my birthday by having a party. Back in those days, we had parties in our houses, not the club. I was too young to get into the club anyway. Our house had a basement so we used it for the party. I needed a DJ so I asked my stepfather's cousin if he could do it. Of course, he said yes and the party started at about 9 pm. The party lasted about 3 hours and when the snacks finished, the people started leaving. One slow song that I liked came on, so I started dancing and the DJ starting dancing with me. He put his arms around my waist and pulled me close.

I was intrigued, and I think I secretly had a crush on him. He was much older than me and he was married, but after that night, we started seeing each other. He was married but separated and that didn't seem to matter to him or me. At the time we started dating, he had a full-time job but he also sold drugs. He was a small-time dealer and his dad was his supplier. This was how I got introduced to drugs. At first, I would say "no," but after a while, I started trying it.

I already knew about marijuana which I used on several occasions, but it just gave me the munchies and made me laugh. This drug was different; it was called cocaine. It was more expensive and had a lasting effect. We started experimenting with it during sex. I remember him putting it on my breast, and it kept me up. We would get high on our supply! He started feeding my habit and I would get the drugs for free.

A few of my friends were experimenting as well but thank God we all were able to put this drug down. My lover never wanted me to work; he wanted us to rely on public assistance. I wanted more out of life than that, so I decided to stop getting high, but I continued my relationship with him. I know God was with me because I was able to stop cold turkey.

Next thing I know, I was pregnant at the tender age of 16! I was young and dumb but still living in my mother's house. I finally found a way to tell my mother that I was pregnant, but it was not easy. We decided that I needed to finish high school, so I had to terminate the pregnancy. We went to the clinic together and I took a pregnancy test (which came back positive). I was confused and scared but not really surprised. I was having unprotected sex and for every action, there is a reaction and consequence. I started to cry and my mother put her arms around me and said: "baby it's ok, I'm here"!

The doctor returned to the room and said you have two options, option one, terminate the pregnancy or option two; keep the baby. The doctor started discussing the procedure for terminating the pregnancy, but something in my spirit said Kim don't do this! God will make a way somehow. We left the clinic that day and decided not to terminate the pregnancy. I knew God had my back as well as my mother. I have never regretted this decision, but it was a turning point in my life.

Juggling school and pregnancy was tough, but my family stepped in to help me as much as they could. My two uncles that I lived with were lifesavers, one worked full-time and the other one was retired. My uncle that was retired volunteered to take care of the baby while I finished high school.

God was watching over the baby and me! I thought I was mature and knew what I wanted out of life. Turns out all I wanted to do was party, skip classes, and hang out with my friends. I had a boy and my son grew up as a grandma's boy. I would often leave him with my mother and go for days at a time.

I believe this was what led my son to make several bad decisions throughout his teenage life. I was not there for him, I was still a teen myself, but that is no excuse.

I thank God every day that I had a wonderful mother, and family who took care of my son and me. I didn't spend my life depending on a man to take care of me but to put my trust in God. Family is everything to me; I don't know where I would be today if it weren't for God and my family. I did things in my past that I am ashamed of but we serve a forgiving God and he never leaves us or forsakes us. He is the "Alpha and Omega"! I had three parents in my life which was an honor but also a challenge. My mother took care of me, my children, and grandchildren all of her life, even until she took her last breath.

Mocha

I grew up with two fathers in my life, but only one raised me and was there for me. There was my biological father, the person who donated his sperm and contributed to my birth who was in and out of my life with broken promises. I wanted to believe

in my biological father, but he always did and said things that were inappropriate or did not have any meaning to me. My mother suffered many years being married to my father and so did I.

14

Leaving my father was one of the most courageous things my mother ever did. Some would call it "running," but if we had stayed, he would have hurt one of us or both of us. Then there is the man who raised me that my mother spent over 30 years of her life with. He was there through the good times and bad. I was young and foolish and didn't have the respect I should have had for him. It wasn't all good in the beginning because I was very jealous and selfish.

It wasn't until years later that I learned to be understanding, loving, and forgiving. My stepfather played a big role in my life and he took care of my mother. If I could do it all over again, I would have respected him more and treated him more like a father. He worked for mass transit most of his career. My stepfather was born and raised in Birmingham, Alabama. He was a large man and was fairly healthy, but he smoked cigarettes. His health failed him in

2008 when he went on to be with the Lord. He was an only child like husband number four.

I remember a time when my stepfather left my mother for another woman. He packed up his stuff and one day decided to move out. He was seeing another woman who had two kids. He met her when he was a Bus Driver. My mother could not have kids and my stepfather was ten years younger than my mother. My mother was strong and God fearing. Although his leaving affected her, she continued to pray and ask God for guidance. My stepfather got laid off from his job, and his car broke down. Could this be a sign that God was telling him that he made a terrible mistake by leaving her? He ended up tucking his head between his tail and running back to her.

My mother had a very forgiving heart and ended up taking him back, but things were never the same between them. I believed they slept together just to comfort one another but not as a couple. They both

16

were fairly large people and I remember teasing my mother about their sex life. She would say "I better get Mikey" which meant her toy. I don't think she actually had one but it used to make me laugh. My parents were married for more than 30 years and are both in heaven now. The cycle of lies, deceit, and adultery continued to plague my life. I asked myself "why" was I being punished for not going to church more, praying to God or not tithing? These are just a few questions that took me until adulthood to get answered.

S'MORES

During my pregnancy, my grandmother on my mother's side was visiting NY for the first time. She was born and raised in South Carolina and was married to my grandfather for over 50 years. I was the oldest granddaughter, so I was the first to make her a great grandmother. She wanted me to have my baby before she left. I started working at a Summer Youth Program while I was pregnant. I did not have a car, so I took the bus every day. I wasn't showing much but my job was easy, so I didn't have to do any heavy lifting or anything.

I remember having a crush on one of the counselors and I think the feeling was mutual. We started having lunch together and just talking about life and our past relationships. He was very kind to me and made me feel special. I guess you could say we liked each other and wanted to spend more time together. I started taking the train to his place in Queens and we would walk, talk, and hold hands. He treated me like a queen and as if he was the father of my baby.

I was pregnant with my son at the time. He was a good listener and friend. A month or so went by and we started getting serious and making plans for the future. We tried to hide our attraction for each other at work, but I think people knew. One day I started getting cramps and feeling sick, so I left work early that day. Later that night, my water broke and I remember my grandmother telling me I was going to have this baby before she went home. My son's father was at the hospital along with my mother. I was in a lot of pain but not ready to deliver. When I got to the hospital, I remember them asking me to breathe, walk, and walk. This was very frustrating because I was ready to meet my baby.

The doctor came into my room and asked me if I wanted an epidural shot for the pain, but I refused because I wanted to have my baby through natural causes. I knew little about it then and if I had to do it all over again, I would have taken the shot!

I was so young and scared, but I knew "God" was going to help me through.

My contractions started getting closer and closer. I went into labor the following morning. My son was born August 9, 1982, the day before I turned 17. He was my birthday present and a gift from God. I remember looking into his eyes and holding his little hand. He was born with a head full of straight jet black hair and one dimple. I did not want the nurse to take him away. I had to get 3 to 4 stitches, but he was healthy and strong. He was 6 lbs. and 10 ounces at birth.

I remember the hospital wanted to keep him one extra day for a procedure called circumcision. I was immature and selfish I did not allow him to stay and get the procedure. If I could go back in time and change that, I would. One thing stuck in my head, I was visited by my friend from the summer job and he brought me flowers. I cried, hugged him and thanked him. After that day, I did not see or speak to him again.

It was like he disappeared from my life. To this day, I still wonder what happened to him. He was my guardian angel and a special guy in my life. After about three days, I took my son home and we settled in. I already had a bassinet and everything he needed. I had a baby shower the month before and I was blessed by my family and friends. It was amazing to me even after I had my baby how small I still was. I was basically "all baby" meaning I didn't pick up any extra weight. So after my first child, I could still wear my stomach out. My mother was there for me through it all. After about two months, I had to think about getting back in school.

French Vanilla

I wanted to finish high school. Living in a house with my aunt, cousins and uncles had its advantages. I was so grateful to my uncle who volunteered to watch my baby so I could finish school. At that time, a lot of girls were dropping out of high school because they were pregnant. I did not want to put a burden on my mother, so I had to make some important decisions. I had to focus and take care of my baby. I am so glad God made a way! I graduated from high school in 1984, but during my last year in high school, I attended classes at a trade school called "BOCES" Board of Cooperative Educational Services which really changed and conditioned my life. I became a "CNA" Certified Nurse's Aide.

I had a job before I graduated and a 450-hour certificate. This was the beginning of a new life for me and my baby. I was able to take care of him and help my family. I kept seeing my baby's father for about a month or two. He wanted me to get on welfare and food stamps. I was stronger than that; I had my whole life ahead of me. My mother taught me to be independent and work hard. I broke up with him later that year.

I met husband number one "French Vanilla" walking home from school one day. He was a year older than me, but I liked him. So I invited him over to my house. I sat next to him on the couch and I remember him moving over, so I moved over, then he moved over again. I guess he was a little shy (RED FLAG). We started seeing each other every week. He would come by after school when my mother was at work, so you know what happened after that. We started having sex, I was about 17, and I already had a son.

I remember my mother coming home from work early and catching us almost in the act! He was standing behind the door when my mother opened it and asked: "who is in here?" He came out from behind the bedroom door and said, "I'm in here Cathy." I thought to myself, did he just do that? Thank God he had his clothes on because that was too close for comfort. I invited him over to my house another day, and my baby's father popped up. He met us sitting in the living room and called me into the bathroom. He slapped me and said, "I was no good and a cheater."

My friend got up because he heard us arguing and asked me if everything was alright? I responded "I'm fine" thank you. At that point, I had to make a decision, did I want to stay with a man who was abusive and sells drugs, or did I want to be with a man who respected me and treated me fairly? The only thing I did not think about was the fact that I did not know enough about my new friend. I chose not to be with my baby's father but to move on to bigger and better things. So I choose to be with my high school sweetheart. The following year we got engaged, and he graduated high school.

He decided to go into the military. His family threw him a barbeque for graduation. I gave him a watch for his graduation, but he broke it because I told him his brother touched me inappropriately (RED FLAG). He had a temper and he pushed me on several occasions. We started using drugs together and fighting. We got married in Washington and we lived there for six months. When I arrived in Washington, we had to stay in a hotel until he could get housing. I remember pawning all my personal belongings just to get a hotel room.

The day I arrived, he bought a car. I did not like living in Washington, it rained every day and there was nothing to do. I made a friend, but she and her husband were constantly arguing and fighting. I would see her on base or at the store and she would have a black eye or bruise. She had two little kids, so I would help her from time to time. I remember calling home and asking my mother to send me a box of stuff like sheets, bathroom products and can goods.

Finally, we moved into housing and started talking about getting married. A few weeks later we got married at the Courthouse. He had two of his friends stand in as witnesses. Marriage was tough and I didn't have a clue about cooking or washing because my mother did everything for me. One time, I made hotdogs for dinner two days in a row, he slapped me with the dishcloth! It seemed like no matter what I did it was not good enough for him. He was always angry and he scared me. I thought to myself, "how in the world did I find myself in the middle of nowhere with a violent man?" He was starting to show his true colors. He was very secretive and liked to disappear at night (Red Flag). Whenever I asked him, he would just say he was working. I knew this was the beginning of a bad relationship.

After a few months, he received his orders to be transferred, so we sold our stuff and packed the car and started on our way to New York. We stopped in a little town in the desert in Kimball Nebraska for breakfast. We were tired and hungry and had been driving all night. As soon as we walked in, everyone turned around and looked at us. We wondered what was going on and went to the counter to order our food while the people were still staring at us.

This was the first time in my life I encountered racism up close and personal. Even though I was afraid, I was with my husband and he was not going to let anything happen to us. Somehow someone from the restaurant called us n****** and my husband and I looked at each other and started for the door. My husband was not afraid and he was ready to fight. We left and went to the nearest gas station and grabbed a few items to eat and drink.

Driving to New York turned out to be a crazy idea because the car ended up breaking down and we had to stay a couple of days in a hotel room. The remaining money we had with us was used to buy bus tickets to New York.

Even though I went through hell in Washington, God was still in control. During my stay, I realized that my husband had a very mean streak and was abusive (RED FLAG). Finally, we made it back to New York, but when my mother saw me, she said I looked horrible as if I had been through hell and back. We ended up moving in with my parents.

My husband received orders to report to Germany. He was not surprised, but I was. This was going to be another separation for us and I was not happy about it. After a couple of weeks, his official orders came and he had to leave. He had never been out of the country before, but he was looking forward to going to Germany. A month went by and we talked a couple of times a week and he wrote me letters. He was homesick and started hanging out. He was getting high with the friends he made there. He was an E4 when he went to Germany but they gave him a urine test, and he failed with two substances in his system. So they pulled his rank, meaning they bussed him down to a private!

He was very upset because we were just about to come to Germany to be with him as a family. He was supposed to get housing, meals, and everything. This hurt me so badly that I started cheating on him and he did the same. He met these two girls who were sisters and he was dating them both. One sister was jealous of the other sister and went to his Commander. She complained against him and he was brought in for questioning. She accused him of forcing her to have sex with him and hitting her. This was a "No No" especially in the military. He was arrested and charged with "blank". He called me and explained to me what had happened. I was in disbelief, upset and in tears.

This was going to put a wedge between us. I prayed about it and wrote a letter to his Commanding Officer asking for his release. Finally, when it was time for him to go to court, the other sister showed up and told the truth. He did not hurt either one of them and he did not "blank" anyone. They released him from jail but discharged him from the military with a "Bad Conduct" discharge for adultery!

He was sent home almost immediately. I was able to forgive him for his indiscretions because I was hurt and doing the same thing. We stayed married, but we still had a lot of issues in our marriage. What we should have done was seek some type of marriage counseling instead of just trying to sweep it under the rug.

Once he arrived home, he started staying out late, hanging out with his friends, and still getting high. He was not able to find a job right away, but after a few months, he found one. I was working with an organization as a helper and I got promoted to work in the office as a secretary. I liked my job, but one day when I was opening the mail, I saw a check with a name on it that I didn't recognize. I thought the person no longer worked for the company. I took the check, signed the back of it with my signature and gave it to the man who cashes checks for the company.

He thought the check was mine until he got to the bank.

This was so illegal on so many levels but I admit "I did it"! I tried to cash another person's check with my signature. Later that day, detectives arrived at my office and asked for me. They read me my Miranda rights, handcuffed me, and took me away. I left with my hands in the air and stomach poking out. I was about eight months pregnant with my daughter. I had never been in trouble with the police before until this day.

I remember arriving at the police station and being asked questions about the check not knowing that signing the back of someone else's check was a "Felony" called "Forgery"! I was scared; I thought I was going to be released once I spoke to my mother and she could bail me out. At first, I started acting like I didn't know what they were talking about, then I asked if I could make a phone call. I called my mother and she told me to tell the truth, so I did. Once I told the truth, the detectives brought me some lunch. I was not going to be released until I went to court which was not going to be until the following morning. So later that day, they placed me in a holding cell which had a toilet and a hard bench.

I was pregnant, so I was tired and didn't want to be there.

Later on that evening, the guards brought a lady into the cell, and she refused to take off her stockings and shoes. It took about three guards to hold her down and take off her stockings and shoes. She was not going to cooperate, and when she looked at me, she said "If I weren't pregnant she would "blank"! All I could do was pray all night. She could have attacked me, or the guards could have hurt me while trying to detain her.

At that point, I asked "God" if he gets me out of this mess, I promise not to do anything like this again! I went to court the following morning with the lawyer my mother got for me. I ended up getting the "Felony" charge reduced to a "Misdemeanor," and I had to pay restitution (meaning pay the money back). I was also placed on probation for a year. I had to learn the hard way but through it all, "God" was right their front and center.

I went to another Trade School and landed a secretarial job. I went through a temp agency, but after a few months, I got a full-time position in Maryland and a relocation package. I had to sign a contract to stay with the company for one full year. Eager to move and be on my own with my family, we had a housewarming party, loaded up the U-Haul truck and moved to Maryland. I enjoyed living in Maryland; I had a two Bedroom two bath apartment. My job was only 15 minutes away and the Mall was down the street. This was the life I always wanted and dreamed of. I even got my husband a position in the mailroom. I believe he was jealous of me and flirted with other women at the job which was disrespectful (RED FLAG).

I was making more money than him and he was always angry. He started leaving at night and coming back late. He kept baking soda in the bathroom and I threw it away every chance I could. He was using drugs again. The drugs had a very distinctive odor, so I knew. I found out he was on drugs by his family before I left New York but I thought I could help him. I wanted to change him. I thought if we relocated and cut our ties, maybe it would help him. He was physically and mentally abusive and became an addict.

I prayed every night and put prayer cloths under the mattress. I went to church, but I was afraid to tell anyone about him or what I was going through. It got so bad that I ended up leaving him and staying in a shelter for battered woman for a few months until I got on my feet. My parents came and picked up my children. I didn't want them to suffer anymore because of me and what I was going through. I was beaten up, talked down too, and controlled. The Shelter helped me put my life back together. I was able to regain my power. I left Maryland and returned to New York, but I was still in love with my husband, so we stayed together.

At the age of 23, I got pregnant with my daughter. My son was about six years old. Several months went by and one day at work, my water broke. I called my husband to pick me up and he rushed me to the hospital. I gave him my purse with my wallet, credit cards, and jewelry. I never saw those items again and he cleaned out my bank account. I was so disappointed in him and hurt. I didn't know what to do, so I continued to pray and ask God for guidance.

In the midst of it all, I was having a baby and the birth of my daughter was one of the greatest times of my life. I really wanted a daughter the first time, but God had a different plan for me. I thought instead of having a child when I was 16 that I should have had my first child at 23. I love my son, but my daughter was like a mini-me! She was premature at birth but healthy and breathing on her own.

I named my daughter after her father's first name and I came up with her middle name. I remember going to the hospital and being in labor with my daughter for 23 hours. When I arrived at the hospital, they wanted me to walk, but I really needed something for the pain. She was not born until the following day, August 13, 1988. I had her 100% natural with no epidural! I had both my children without any anesthesia. She was born with a head full of hair and she looked exactly like her father. She was born at 4 lbs. and had to stay in the hospital because she was premature.

At the time of her birth, my son for some reason threw up on the floor at the hospital. We still don't know why or what happened but at the exact moment, he did. Thinking this would be a turning point in our lives, I wanted to save my marriage, but he was still mean and abusive. On several occasions, he pushed me and one time he put his foot on me when I was pregnant. I don't think he meant to hurt me, but he did. So here I am at the hospital with my newborn baby girl, and the doctor comes into my room to tell me that I will have to get a shot before I leave. I said to myself, a shot for what? He said PID (Pelvic inflammatory disease).

My husband had infected me, but thank God it was not passed on to the baby! Two days went by, and I did not see my husband. I did not want him to pick me up from the hospital, so I called one of my closest friends. Once I got home, I settled in with the baby. After about a week, my husband finally came home and saw the baby. I remember us arguing and I ran out of the house. My mother followed me out and we got into the car. He jumped on the hood of the car and cracked the windshield. My life continued to spiral out of control and my husband needed help with his drug addiction and abuse.

After several years of pain and hardship, I finally divorced him. I was married to him for seven years, and he finally entered rehab to get the help he needed. While he was in rehab, I divorced him. I needed a clean start and my parents wanted to be closer to their parents, so we relocated as a family to Atlanta, GA.

I actually moved a few months before my parents. I lived with my cousin for a few months. We used to party every weekend and go from club to club. She took care of the kids during the week. My cousin was a couple of years older than me, but we hit it off right away. She taught me a lot about foreign men meaning she only dated men from other countries. So of course, I got on the bandwagon.

I started dating an African man from West Africa. We dated a few months and moved in together. He was a great guy; he taught me about African food and how to make "Fu Fu." He would speak to my mother from time to time when she called. He promised her he would take care of me until they arrive. We stayed together for a couple of months, but we loved to party.

We started partying every weekend. One night, he didn't come home. I was so worried by the time he got home I was gone. I went looking for him and calling all of our friends to see if they had seen him. So the next thing I thought was he was with another woman. In a jealous rage, I called one of my friends and drove to his place. I started drinking and smoking marijuana. My judgment was clouded but I was feeling good. We were listening to music, and we started dancing, kissing, and one thing led to another.

A few hours passed, and I decided to get dressed and go home. When I got to the door, my boyfriend was standing there with tears in his eyes. It was as if he already knew what I had done before I could tell him. He just kept saying "what did you do"? I started crying, and things were never the same between us after that day, but he promised my mother, so he kept his promise. A year later, my cousin was murdered by her boyfriend and I miss her so much. She didn't deserve to leave this earth like that. I am still in contact with her daughters and family. My parents moved down a few months later. I was starting to get homesick and my kids were with my parents. I loved them very much but at that time I was not working and I was living with my cousin so I left them with my parents.

I was starting my life over and did not want them to see my struggles. I always wanted them to be in a safe and stable environment. After a couple of months, my parents moved to Atlanta. They moved into a three bedroom apartment, and we all lived together. I lived with my parents for about two years and then I got my apartment.

RASPBERRY SWIRL

My daughter was in her senior year in college when she got pregnant with my granddaughter. She was born three months early weighing 1 lb. 11 ounces which was severely premature. We call her our "Miracle Baby," we thank God every day that she made it through. The last thing on my daughter's mind was dating. She met a young man through a friend of hers. She met this young man when she was very vulnerable and had gone through a tough time. They started seeing each and going out together.

After a few months, they got really serious and moved in together. She co-signed with him on an apartment and a vehicle. She seemed happy and content, but I saw signs of things that didn't seem right. I remember asking her on several occasions was everything ok and she would say yes mom things are fine. I knew in my heart and spirit that something was wrong. She would not confide in me because she was very secretive and kept things to herself. I think she didn't want people to know her business.

This was a pattern for me and the women in my family, a cycle of destructive control by men. Her boyfriend was secretly demeaning and abusive both physically and mentally. I remember her telling me a story about his abuse. They were riding in the car together and she said something that he did not like so he slapped her. She hit the back of another car, but there was no damage to the other car, thank God.

He threw things at her and liked to fight her. She felt she had no one to turn to; her grandmother had passed on. I was her mother but I was wrapped up in my own mess, and I regret not being there for her. If I had to do it all over again, I would always be there for my children no matter what!

I am so glad she was able to break free from this man and move on with her life.She is now happily married and has two daughters. She got her Bachelors Degree and she is teaching full time. It did not take her but one time to get it right. She is now working on her Masters' Degree. I am so proud of my daughter; she is a mother, wife, sister, aunt, mentor, and educator.

Judge

My son was a whole other story. He was kicked out of public school and was sent to Alternative School because he was playing with a knife on the school bus and nearly cut a girl. I believe if the School Board had thought that he maliciously did it, he would have been sent to juvenile, but the Judge asked if I wanted him to go to Reform School and I said no. I wonder if his life would have turned out differently today if I didn't let him go. He ended up dropping out of high school and hanging around the wrong crowd. He started robbing people and then decided to rob the local store where he buys his cigarettes.

I am not sure where this behavior came from but we always gave our son things on a silver platter, and I believe this was part of the problem. He was spoiled and a grandma's boy! One day, I received a call from the DeKalb County Detectives Division. They asked me questions about my son's whereabouts and that they had a few more questions to ask him.

They wanted to come by the house and speak with him in person. I was scared and didn't know what to do. As a mother, I was confused about what to do at that point, whether to hide him or let him speak with the detectives. So I called my husband at the time and he told me not to let him make a statement without a lawyer. I wish I had listened to his advice, but I didn't.

My son came home and I spoke with him about the phone call I received. I asked him to tell the truth and repent of his sins. The Detectives arrived to question him and he got on his knees and told the truth (confessed his sins). On that day, they arrested my son and took him into custody, and he had to appear before a judge. I had to think quickly; he needed a lawyer. At the time, I was working for a law firm and I thought of asking my employer to represent my son (Red Flag). He was not a criminal attorney but a domestic attorney.

My son was charged with three felonies, but only two stuck. He spent ten years of his life in the jail system. It was horrifying and I will never forget that day in court. Tears rushed down my eyes when the judge said "10 years with no chance of parole"! It was as if I was in prison with him. He was only 16 years old, and he did not get out until he was 26.

It has been hard for my son to get a job with two felonies on his record. I always had high hopes and dreams for my firstborn son. He has made me the proud grandmother of two. Sometimes I feel that he is bitter about what happened to his life. I blame myself in some ways because I was a young mother and I should have put his needs first. I didn't have a childhood; I was forced to grow up fast. I was doing grown-up things at a very early age.

$\mathcal{P}$EPPERMINT

I enrolled in a 2-year college and I was going to major in Nursing, but I decided to go with Business instead. My English Professor was very interesting and I enjoyed the course. I met husband number two "Peppermint" at a local college.

He was very clean cut and always put on his uniform. I invited him and a few classmates out for a drink after class. He approached me and I looked up, he was very tall. He asked me where we were going and who is going? I simply said "It's just me" and he said ok, let's meet in the parking lot, and decide where to go. So we went to a restaurant close to the school. We ordered two drinks, but he was surprised because I picked up the tab. He looked shocked, but we exchanged numbers and began talking.

We dated for about six weeks and got serious really fast. He wanted me to move in with him. I was not ready for that, but he talked me into it. We moved in together with his sister and her kids. Our living arrangements were very hard with so many in one apartment. Finally, we moved into a house next to his parents and grandmother. This husband was a chef (in his mind), and I didn't have to cook or shop, he did it all. I was very spoiled, but we had other issues in our marriage. We had a blended marriage, meaning he had a son from a previous marriage and I had my two kids.

I was angry about my son being in prison, and I felt like I was in prison too. When I found out my son had been robbing people, it hurt me to my heart. That was not how we raised him; he didn't need anything. I still to this day don't understand why. My husband and I did not agree on the outcome of the case. He felt my son should be locked up for his crimes and I was angry about it. He would not visit my son or speak with him. He was intelligent, a great cook and a hard worker.

We had a couple of issues in this marriage though. One very important issue was sex, he had a fetish for anal sex. I thought I was obligated to fulfill his fantasies because he was my husband. I grew bitter and angry all the time because I did not want to do this type of sex. He was a fairly tall man with a small package, so he called me out on his fetish honeymoon night. I will never forget that night; I cried and cried. It was one of the worst nights of my life which was supposed to be one of the happiest.

I was so frustrated and upset all the time, so I started going online and chatting with people. I should have taken my problems to God. Another important issue for us was finance. We started getting payday loans or borrowing from his family. Things got very tight, and we ended up separating in the same house. I came home one day and discovered that he had moved the bed to his grandmother's house. So I moved my daughters' bed to our room.

The following day, I came home from work and the lights and water were turned off manually! That was the last day I lived in the house. I loaded everything I could into my car and moved. I remember throwing all the bears he had given me over the years out on the lawn and his mother picked them up. I was angry, but I wanted to leave more than ever. He was smug and confident that I would leave. I moved to another county and even though I lived in another county, we were still seeing each other and sleeping with each other.

One day I decided to stop by the house during my lunch hour and he was outside working on his car. He looked up at me, but all I could see was "blood" in his eyes. I thought we were being civil to each other because he would bring my mail to my job, and we would talk from time to time, but I was wrong. He decided to go down to the courthouse and take out a warrant against me. He claimed he did not know my address and so he had the officers come to my job. They presented me with the warrant and walked me through the parking lot to their vehicle.

The officers were actually nice about it; they did not cuff me until I got in the vehicle. I ended up spending one night in jail. When I was arrested, I almost had all the bond money on me, but I was short. So I did not get out until the following day. The judge threw out the charges and requested that we do mediation. After mediation, we divorced. Our marriage lasted four years and he divorced me due to irreconcilable differences. He went his way and I went mine.

$\mathcal{L}$ATTE

I had a debate with my brother this year on how old I am. It was really funny he told me to do the math, I've been telling people that I am 51, but I am actually 52! I had my daughter Sanaa at the age of 41. Imagine my surprise; my older children are ages 35 and 29. I have an 11-year old girl born August 6, 2006. She is very special, but I also knew she was different. We lived in DeKalb County for a couple of years and I was in denial about her behavior. The teachers were calling me every week about how she was acting in class. I just thought it was immaturity. I even went up to the school, checked her out and spanked her in the restroom, checked her back in school and let her go back to class.

I was a very tough "no-nonsense" mother! I was raised by a parent who did not spare the rod! So I grew up with high standards and good morals. Finally, after making an appointment and having her tested for ADHD, we knew the truth. She started off taking 15 mg, and as she got older, we raised it every year. She takes up to 25 mg once daily each month. She has trouble sleeping at times, so the doctor recommended an over-the-counter medicine for sleeping. At times her appetite is very low and she only eats certain things. I pray to God daily that one day she will outgrow this ADHD nightmare. She is very intelligent and strong. Her grades are all A's with an occasional B. I thank God every day for her and I know why God gave me a baby at 41.

I was devastated when I lost my mother, but I had my baby to help me focus and try to move on with my life. Burying my mother was one of the hardest things I ever had to do in my life! She would have wanted me to carry on the legacy of the family, take care of the children and the grandchildren. I always wanted my mother to be proud of me, and one of the things I know she would have wanted me to do is finish college. I started college in 2007, it is now 2017, and I have six classes left to graduate! Attending school part-time was a struggle, but it is definitely worth it. I want my grandchildren and children to see me walk across that stage.

ALMOND JOY

I met husband number three "Almond Joy" online! What was I thinking? I was not thinking with my "head" on top if you get my drift. I should have learned my lesson about dating online but I was lonely and I worked a lot. I had two children at the time and my hands were always full. I started joining websites online, and one site, in particular, stood out. I would review profile after profile, look at pictures, and decide who to leave a message for. Finally, husband number three, tall, gorgeous eyes, and packing (and I don't mean clothes)! I had a passion for men with large wheels if you know what I mean. He was living in Alpharetta with his sister and her son. They were in business together, and he worked from home.

We started talking on the phone a lot and sending pictures, and finally, we met in person. I invited him over to my apartment. We had a few drinks and one thing led to another. Before we actually had sex, he whispered something into my ear "If we go down this road, there is no turning back, are you sure?" I was not sure what to think of that, but I was tipsy and horny at the same time. In my mind, I believe that same night I got pregnant with my third child. We dated for a few months and then he popped the question. We moved in together and I missed a period, so I knew I was pregnant.

This was a miracle from God! I was 41 years old when I had my second daughter. She is the best thing that came out of that marriage because her dad and I only stayed married for eight months. We separated before she was born. He was a cheater and an alcoholic. I learned to never judge a book by its cover, for example, his teeth was a plate, he had an accident and had to have all his teeth removed!

He would pop the plate in and out of his mouth like it was nothing, but they looked real (RED FLAG). God showed me early on that this was not the man for me. He was not abusive, but we argued a lot. He did not have a car (RED FLAG), but I did. I always thought third time's a charm, but not in my case. This marriage lasted nine months and I divorced him. He moved back to New York and I was awarded child support and sole custody.

$\mathcal{P}$UMPKIN $\mathcal{S}$PICE

I met "Pumpkin Spice" online but he was one of the coolest guys I have ever met online. He has his own business, place to stay and several cars. He is definitely my kind of guy! What I remember most about him is his great sense of humor and honesty. We casually started chatting online and sending each other pictures. He invited me out, and I could not wait to meet him face to face. I knew I was taller than him from his profile but that did not matter to him, he liked that about me. He also would give me several compliments on my lips.

He was a straight gentleman and made me feel welcome. When he came to the door, he looked just like his pictures, handsome. I went upstairs and got my coat; I rode with him. He opened the door for me and that was nice. We went to a club and had a couple of drinks. I remember him asking me to dance. He got up and we started dancing, I was so surprised because he could actually dance. He was very sexy and he had this deep southern voice that made me melt.

He was a few years older than me but he out-danced me. I was sweating trying to keep up with him. We stayed at the club for a couple of hours and then we left. He brought me home and walked me to the door. I invited him in but he said it was late, so he kissed me and left. We starting talking on the phone more and getting to know each other. I invited him over for dinner the next time. I remember introducing him to my mother and she thought he was nice.

I had been through a lot, so my mother didn't make any comments about him until after he left. I entertained him in the den; we had wings and a glass of wine. He looked so cute that night; he was wearing a nice dress shirt with jeans. I remember his jeans creased as if he sent them to the cleaners. He always smelled so good; he was different from most men. This was the beginning of something really special. Could this be the "One" not sure but it felt so right.

We continued to date but I went out of town one week and I mentioned a few things I did while I was away. One of the things I did was smoking marijuana with my friends which was not normal for me, but I was having fun. It's not like I was a drug addict, but it completely turned my friend off. I guess sometimes what happens in Vegas should stay in Vegas. He was very surprised and he let me know that was not cool. He stopped calling me and we didn't go out anymore. I could not understand why he dumped me until now. He let me know that he felt very strongly about drugs and did not want to be a part of that scene.

CA-RA-MEL

I lived with a friend for several months after my daughter was born, but I ended up moving back home. My parents were living in an apartment at that time. After a couple of years, we bought a home together, five bedrooms and three full baths. My stepdad became ill, and he passed away before we moved. My stepdad wanted to be buried in the family plot. He was originally from Alabama and was married to my mother for over 30 years. After moving into this home, we realized we had all this space and it was just me, my mother and youngest daughter.

My oldest daughter was in college and my son incarcerated. I was very spoiled by my mother. She was an angel on earth! It hurts me to my heart every day that is gone, but I know God needed her more! She was my rock, but she was battling breast cancer. She had a mastectomy after being diagnosed one year later. My mother helped everybody, whether they needed a place to stay or food.

Financially, my mother always had it together; I wish I could have been more like her. The sad part is we all drained her, but she loved us and didn't know how to tell us no. She loved all of us equally, but I believe my first born was her favorite. My mother raised my son because I was too young to understand and I stayed in the streets. My son got released from prison in 2008, but my mother was diagnosed with cancer.

I remember that day so clearly in my mind because it was one of the happiest days of my life. I had my family all together under one roof. My youngest daughter and my mother were road dogs; they went everywhere together. My oldest daughter would come home to visit from college especially during holiday time. She adored her grandmother and is so much like her financially and spiritually.

If I could turn back the hands of time and go back to when we first moved into the house, I would. My mother had a heart of gold, and I was her only daughter. I have two brothers who were raised by my grandparents in South Carolina. Before my mother died, she stayed in the hospital for two weeks with pneumonia. After she got out, she was in stage four of breast cancer.

During the time my mother was ill, I had a live-in boyfriend who was my lover. He was a great help to my family and me. He would help me feed my mother and change her. We dated for few weeks and he moved in. My mother was fond of him because he would run errands for her or anything she needed he would get it. Eventually, we had to get a nurse to come in while we worked full-time. This was one of the toughest things we had to do because my mother took care of people all her life. We were blessed with a nurse from one of the agencies she worked for.

When she passed on, I received a call from the Director at the agency; she was calling to tell me not to worry about the bill! My God, all I could do was cry and thank him.

We had a nurse for about six weeks. One day after I came home from work, I went in to check on her, and her sugar had spiked all the way up to 400. We called 911 and followed the ambulance to the hospital. The doctor came into the room and told us to gather all the family together to come to the hospital that she may not make it through the night. I left and went home to grab my clothes so I could spend the night at the hospital.

I was so scared, but I knew God was there. I remember walking into the room and she had an oxygen mask on her face and she kept pulling the mask down like she was ready to go. My oldest brother did not want to let go so he kept putting the mask back on. I slept on the couch next to the bed. The nurse came in that night to change her position and make her comfortable. I kissed her on her forehead and prayed with her.

The next morning, the doctor came in and started walking toward me and said she's gone! I jumped up and ran over to her bedside and held her for as long as I could. I cried for several days, I just wanted her back. After a couple of days, I was able to talk with my family and make funeral arrangements. My mother passed on May 9, 2010, which was a Sunday and Mother's Day. God had called her home, no more pain.

My mother was everything to all of my family. She was the glue that held us all together. She taught me how to love and forgive people. She was there for me, the children, and grandchildren. She cooked for us, kept the house clean and never asked us for anything in return. She was a saint and is still with us in spirit! If she was still here on this earth, what would she say to me about this book?

I believe in my heart she would say "baby tell your story" help people to know "God's" word, teach our ladies to wait on their "Boaz" and live their lives through him. I hear her plain as day and I will meet her at the "Pearly Gates" of heaven.

After the death of my mother, I was depressed and started going online joining the yahoo groups. I started emailing and connecting with people; then I met a guy who was into swinging. I had no idea what was in store for me. I started going to different types of parties and most of the time, the people at the parties were half naked. This was standard at the swing parties. I ended up going to a swing club that was so different. When you walk in, the club is set up like a regular club, except you bring your own brown bag and they serve it to you. Dance floor and stripper pole with a mirror. Go past the dance floor and there was a room with lockers in it. You could not go past this point with clothes on. In the lockers were towels for you to wear around or you had to wear a teddy of your own.

Swinging was state of the art. Either you are or not and just watched. During my first two visits, I just watched in amazement. I saw people walking around butt naked. People were having sex in rooms and there was a bar where people were having sex on the couch in front of the bar. Oh and the orgy rooms where couples have sex with each other out in the open, no holds bar. My eyes were always open and my mouth was too. I was not used to seeing this type of stuff. I did not think I could do this or fit in, but I actually participated more than once. Couples were always attracted to me and they wanted to get with me. I started having parties at my house and charging a fee to get in. I remember having a limo in my driveway and people in the limo having sex. We had bowls of condoms and informed people about the need to be careful and to enter at their own risk.

$\mathcal{C}$HOCOLATE

Let me start by saying "Chocolate" was a close, close friend but not a husband, he was a lover. I think if I had to do it all over again, I should have married him. We met when I was selling movies; he was my first customer. He bought like 50 movies and I was impressed. We started talking on the phone and seeing each other from time to time. He invited me out on a date finally, but he was a little mysterious. I found out why; he was married.

I was single and dating, but he was tall, handsome, and intelligent. I was so attracted to him that we started spending a lot of time together. Even though he was married, he was with me all the time, any time! He dressed very sexy and treated me like a queen. I was spoiled, but he was married. We would meet in special places like restaurants or clubs. He always kept a flask filled with something to drink in it.

We always had fun no matter where we were or what we did. He always kept me on edge, especially in the bedroom. I knew I was committing a sin but at that time in my life, I was a sinner. I asked God for forgiveness daily. Even though he was married, he was not happily married. So I thought maybe I might have a chance. We dated for like four years off and on. He desperately wanted a child and his wife could not have any, so he turned to me. I didn't want any children at that time, but I was in love and I wanted him to be happy. I remember him paying my copay and going with me to the doctor to see what chance I would have to get pregnant. I had an IUD when I met him, but he wanted me to have it removed.

I had several tests done that day, so we had to wait for the result. The doctor wanted to tell me the result in person and he went with me. The results came back as I had a very small percentage of getting pregnant. He was excited about the results and started making plans for the baby and me. I was scared but I wanted to make him happy, so I kept trying and trying.

After three years, he finally got his divorce. I was so happy but still no pregnancy. He didn't want to give up, but it just didn't happen. After four years of dating, I wanted more than just having fun with no strings attached. We were close but that was not enough for me. I wanted to get married again and buy a home. He was divorced but not ready to jump back into the arena and that is when I met "Hazelnut"!

ℋAZELNUT

Last but not least, husband number four. Yes, I met him online too! Hazel eyed nut; I came up with that name because of his eyes and personality. You would have thought I would have learned my lesson about online dating. I wanted a fresh start and he seemed quiet and country (RED FLAG). So here I am middle-aged, three kids, two grown adults on their own and one still in the nest. I was divorced and dating again which I thought the third time was a charm.

We started off kind of slow, just talking on the phone and sending each other pictures. One night, I invited him over for dinner but he told me he didn't have a car (RED FLAG) so he took the bus. He did have a job working at a grocery store, but he was living with his aunt (RED FLAG). I ignored all the flags and started inviting him over more and more. Next thing I know, he moves in with me. He told me he was 38, but I later found out he was only 32 when I met him (RED FLAG). After about one year, we got married. We went down to the justice of the peace and had a big reception later on. This husband was shy and didn't have any friends (RED FLAG). He was battling with several health conditions that he failed to reveal to me at the beginning (RED FLAG). He was drinking, battling depression and Crohn's disease.

After four years of marriage, he is now stating that when he met me, he was a virgin. He didn't tell me that to my face; he left me two voicemails (RED FLAG). I saw all the signs but ignored them all. You could not tell me anything because I was in love. All my friends tried to warn me and say "There is something wrong with him," but once again I chose to ignore the flags. I almost fell out with one of my closest friends because I did not take too kindly to her telling me he was "crazy."

This husband was different in some ways from the other husbands, but in other ways, he had major issues. He was a storyteller and he made up several stories. He told me he was married before. He lied about his age and his date of birth. He told me he was having sex with one of his professors in college.

I wanted things to be right, so I believed him, and I wanted our marriage to work.

All my other marriages, I ran from one man to another. He once told me that "he knew he couldn't get a woman like me without making up a character." We have been married for four years going on to five years as of today. I am still married to husband number four, but we are separated and I had to put him out. I could not take it anymore! He was keying my car, throwing away my clothes and wrecked one of my vehicles on purpose.

These are just a few things since I decided not to discuss everything. He has asked me to forgive him, but I am still hurt and disappointed. I was always taught that you don't bite the hand that feeds you. I took care of this man for four years. We discussed couples therapy and spiritual counseling, but I don't see that coming to pass. I don't know whether this marriage will stand the test of time or if this marriage was ordained by "God." I do know I am not going to continue down this path of betrayal, deceit, and mistrust.

I learned that if you don't have trust in your marriage, you don't have a marriage. We have been separated for almost two years but are you still in the same place we left off? I asked myself if I want to stay or run. Running from husband to husband is something that I have done over the past few marriages. When I look in the mirror daily, what do I see? A woman who is intelligent, hardworking and saved, not perfect. It's like being on a plane in "first class," but he is stuck in "coach." I do not think I am better than the next woman, but I have learned so many things on this journey.

His journey is beginning to draw him closer to God and he wants to be a Minister. He is going to school now and trying to change his life, but that does not mean we were meant to be. I see him from time to time and I talk with him on the phone. He has come a long way from where he was a year ago. We have been separated for a year and I have started divorce proceedings. Still praying to God for understanding, forgiveness, and guidance.

I spent the last four years, going on to five with a man I thought was "The One"! I asked myself, did I even know him? Did we do what most couples do, meet and jump in the bed? The answer to these questions is yes! Was I so desperate to be with a man or so lonely that I just didn't care? Did I leave my beliefs and principles at the door? He had all the qualities I desire in a man but that does not constitute a marriage. How do I pick up the pieces of my life and start over? My oldest daughter challenged me to not be in a serious relationship for one full year and I took her up on the challenge not to mention I am celibate. I asked her if I could have friends and she said absolutely!

After being married four times, what is in store for marriage number five? Am I taking baggage from the previous marriages? I believe in my heart and spirit that God will place a wonderful God-fearing, family-loving, and age-appropriate man in my life. I have to wait and stop letting my flesh get in the way.

I don't want to stay married this 4th time especially if there are no changes. Dating has changed since I first started. When I first started dating, I would spot a guy that I liked and we would strike up a conversation and exchange numbers.

With the advancement of technology in the 21st century, we do everything online. Doing everything online is much easier and you can send pictures, exchange telephone numbers but you really don't know if what you see is what you are going to get. It seems that guys are only after one thing and if this is true I am here to let them know that I am celibate. My body is the temple of God, and I will not break my vows until I remarry a 5th time.

Online dating is what it is. It's like you have to cross your fingers and close your eyes and hope you pick a needle out of a haystack! Lately, my luck has not been good because I've met guys from other states, countries and they don't seem to have anything to talk about. I even have spoken with the parent of one of the guys I met online. I realized that this is not the way, so I canceled my account. I don't want to be alone, but I don't want to make the wrong decision again! This time, I have my priorities in order, and the stakes are high! I have taken on the cliché "My way or the highway"!

I don't want to penalize other men for what others have done to me in the past, but I will stand strong and not compromise my integrity or my belief in God!

*C*INNAMON

Question is would I do it a 5th Time? I asked myself that question over and over again in my mind. I believe my answer would be "Yes." God has taught me the error of my ways and how to break the cycle! First, I have to put my trust in him, believe he will change me, and continue to follow his word. Stop trying to find a husband and let my husband find me. I was so tired of being abused, hurt, and let down. This was my breaking point; enough was enough. I just wanted to be happy and grow in Christ.

I remember a time in my life where I almost lost my life. My oldest daughter who is now 29, has two daughters. Her 1st daughter was born a preemie (1lb, 11 ounces). We did a lot of praying for her because she was so tiny. She stayed in the hospital for three months. We finally got a call from her doctor to say she was ready to come home, so we began to celebrate. Instead of getting on our knees in a Church somewhere, we decided to go out for drinks. We went to a sports bar and had about 2 to 3 drinks, but these were very strong drinks.

My daughter called her best friend and she met us at the bar. So we were dancing, singing, drinking, and having fun. The time was about 1 am, so we left the bar and wanted to party some more, but my daughter had left her ID at home. So we headed home to get the ID. It was already like 2 am by then, so we should have just turned in.

We got back in my SUV and headed to the club. I drove down a side street and stopped at the stop sign. I was going to make a left turn when I heard the train siren and lights started to blink. The arm on the train started to come down. In my mind, I wanted to get across the tracks before the arm got all the way down. I proceeded to race against the train. My judgment was way off, and I was tipsy. I got all the way up on the tracks and more than halfway over them when I was hit by the train across the back of the SUV.

The truck spun out about two times and opened up in the back like a sardine can. The airbags deployed, we were scared and dizzy. We had no idea what the damage was until we stumbled out of the vehicle. I called 911 and the police came and we explained what happened. We all went to the emergency room and got checked out. A couple of hours later we were released to go home. My truck was impounded, but I wanted to get my things out.

I called the towing company and they told me that with ID and registration, I could get my stuff. When I arrived to get my stuff all I could do was cry.

God had given me, my daughter, and her best friend a second chance to live. Looking at that SUV and being hit by a train going who knows how fast, I was obvious that God saved us! Not only did I put my life in danger but the lives of my daughter and her friend. I had to drop to my knees and ask for forgiveness. I learned several valuable lessons especially not to drink and drive. The police questioned us and it just never came up about the drinking. Once again God continues to prove that even though we were dead wrong, he still protected us.

There was one other occasion where I was traveling to South Carolina for a holiday with the family. It was me, my mother and my oldest daughter. We often liked to travel and visit with family. We stayed in South Carolina for two days, and we were returning on the highway. We started singing and playing the music loudly. I was driving, it was drizzling, and I guess I was a little tired.

All of a sudden, I swerved and ended up on the median. I remember my mother screaming out "Jesus," Father God! We almost ran in the back of someone; it was a miracle that we missed them. My mother was a strong believer and she went to Church most Sundays. She taught us everything she could about God, helping others and praying. She was like an angel on earth and any family who came to Georgia stayed with us. I know God wanted her up there with him. This is another example of God covering us with his power and blood. I can honestly say I have had nine lives, 4 husbands, 3 divorces, 2 friends, 1 God!

JOFFEE

Just when I thought I could not find love again, poof he appears online. Yes I started online dating again. He sent me a note and we began conversing. He is single, never been married and has his own place. Most guys marry at least once, but he was different. He had a little country tone but he is from up North which is cool because so am I. We sent each other pictures and enjoyed communicating with each other. He lives about 35 to 40 minutes away, we have not met in person yet but I am looking forward to it. He has kind eyes and big feet, so I think I know the package is tight. Men like to fool us woman; they tell us what they think we want to hear.

I am a confident woman but at times I can get lonely. I know God is with me, but my flesh wants to be in a relationship. There are so many things to a relationship and being intimate is just one part. Communication plays a big role in establishing a good repor with each other. Taking time to get to know each other is one effective way of knowing if this could work or not. We also have to put our trust in God and let his decision stand, especially if he shows you the signs. As a woman, we need to be aware of the signs.

We talked on the phone a few times and I started to notice that certain times of night I could not get a hold of him (Red Flag). He told me he lived with a friend in their basement (Red Flag). He said he had a job as a mover and he owned the company but was trying to change fields (Red Flag). I was not trying to cast any judgment but I have been down this road several times.

He came by my place one evening bearing gifts since I invited him. He had three small red bags in his hand. To my surprise, it was perfume and lotion which he knew from our previous conversations that I liked this type of stuff. I thanked him and I asked if he bought them from a certain store. He said no that he already had these items (Red Flag).

So you are saying you are between jobs, living arrangements suspect and I can't reach you from time to time. I saw these flags a mile away and I cut this off so fast it because it would have made your head spin! I blocked his phone number and text messages. I keep continuously learning the hard way because I am not a patient person. I know God will provide all. I just have to roll up my sleeve, put on my big girl pants, and wait! I am still in the healing process and I am not sure what will be next for me but I will be graduating from college, writing a book and developing my organization.

$\mathcal{C}$ONCLUSION

My life was filled with people who loved me as well as people who hurt me. I learned through my prayers and church that "God" is first. My Church taught me to pray, tithe, fast and witness. I am so glad I finally met "God" up close and personal. Without "him" I would have been long gone. I realized that finding a husband was not the correct path but waiting for "God" to send him to me is what I missed. Breaking the chain or curse which is what it was called back when I was little is what kept me going. I survived abuse, mental and spiritual warfare. I know my mother and father are watching over me and God is still in control of my life.

One day I was driving home from school and my gas gauge said 39 miles till empty. I hit my GPS to see how far it was from the school and it said 38 miles away. I wondered if I was going to make it. I started to get a little worried, so I called my youngest daughter to let her know I may have to stop for some gas. I decided to go down the main hwy instead of the back road like I normally do, but it was late and dark. I stopped at a gas station a little less than halfway home. I started praying and talking to God, I had two credit cards, one of the cards had a negative balance and the other one didn't have enough on it to get gas.

While I was talking on the phone with my daughter, I kept praying "Lord I know you're not going to leave me on the side of the road." So I got back in the car and started traveling down the road and I got to another main hwy and my warning light came on indicating 3 miles till empty. I started praying again, then I heard and felt a shake like God had put his hand on the car and was telling me I was going to make it! I kept driving and the next thing I knew, I was three blocks from my house and then two blocks from my house and I finally pulled up in front of my door.

My daughter was so happy; she was downstairs waiting for me. I pulled up and said, "Thank you Lord"!

This was my testimony, not only did I make it home with no bars on the tank, I was able to start the car up the following morning and make it to the gas station with no problem. Nothing but my God took care of me that day. He is a way maker out of no way! I could testify all day and every day. My current vehicle (the one that did not stop) is a blessing. My son told me about a man who was a gm at a dealership he knew. I went online and applied for a vehicle. I was excited because I found a vehicle that was great on gas and easy on the eyes, sporty.

I was blessed with this car for no money down and my payment was the lowest I ever had.

My due date was close to the end of the month, and I still got ten days past that with a late fee of only $5. This vehicle was delivered by God all the way from Massachusetts early in the morning before I went to work. I tipped the driver $20 just for getting it to me before work. He unloaded the vehicle and I signed the paperwork. I got in the vehicle and realized it was touchscreen, sunroof, leather seat, push button start and I had a full tank of gas! Look at God; this was my miracle car. I have not had any problems with the car yet! I called the dealer back and thanked him over and over again. This deal was closed in less than 30 days.

Time after time, God continues to guide me and teach me to help other people.

I was at QT getting my normal cappuccino and donut. I was sitting outside in my car and I noticed a family, a mom, a dad and about four kids waiting outside of QT trying to get an Uber. God whispered into my ear to give that family a lift, so I rolled my window down and I asked the mother where they needed to go? She said "They were headed to an elementary school up the street" it was the first day of school. I loaded everybody up in my one little small Honda Civic and we headed to the school. Once we got to the school, everybody got out and the mother thanked me and she wanted to offer me money but I refused to take it. When God tells you to do something, you do it with no questions asked. I was able to get to work on time with no problem.

I remember a day I was at Cato's on my lunch hour and I was in there shopping for a few items. I was in the dressing room area trying on clothes and I

97

came out and heard a lady at the register trying to pay for her items. For some reason, her card kept declining because the amount was very small. I asked her how much it was and the cashier said $6.50, so I took out my debit card and I swiped it on the keypad. I saw the lady's face as her eyes lit up like gold, she hugged me so tight and thanked me and that moment remained fresh in my mind and my spirit for days.

One day I was heading to the bank and I saw a young lady and God said; ask her if she needs a ride. She looked at me and I looked at my daughter, she said "yes please" she was heading in the same direction we were. When she got in the car, she started talking. She said she was really tired and did not feel like walking and God sent me as an angel to give her a ride. She lived in the same complex as us.

This was just another thing God asked me to do, and I was obedient. It is important that we listen and obey God's word. Life is not just about ourselves; it's about giving back and helping others. I am a tither and I give offerings, but I believe in God and I do it out of the kindness of my heart. When the spirit of God moves you, he guides you on how and what to do for others.

Through the humbleness that God has shown me, taught me, and kept me from my flesh, I will forever be at God's mercy. Yesterday, I had the opportunity to attend an interview for a security position. I was a little nervous but I knew God had my back, so I didn't let it show. I was working part-time for a Pizza Company as a delivery driver for the last two months and things were not working out, so I resigned one Saturday.

I went to this interview with an open mind and heart; I answered all the questions the employer asked me. I felt confident and the manager informed me that he would give me an answer by not later than the following day. My phone rang at about 8 p.m. and I looked at my caller ID, it was the manager from the security company. He was calling to offer me the position starting with training and paid double-digit weekly salary.

All I could do was praise God because he told us if we do his will, help other people and love one another, he will provide for us. So what this means to me is that it's better to give than receive and when one door closes, two or three new doors open. Not only was I offered one position, but God blessed me with three positions. I have to choose the one that he wants me to do.

I started working for a security company at a local mall. A few of the stores have private security, meaning 1 or 2 officers in their particular store. I had training with the manager, but I didn't realize I would be on my feet the whole shift. A typical shift was 6 hours long with two 15 min breaks. If you worked 8 hours, you would receive 60 min lunch and one 15 minute break. The uniform for the company was all black with a tie, very similar to "Men in

Black;" the manager used that as an analogy. I felt uncomfortable dressed like a man but it was a part of the job and it was paying well. On my first day, I arrived at the store and the manager was standing outside of the store with the doors locked.

I thought this was strange since the store usually opens at 9 am. I asked the manager what was happening. He said an employee knocked down the fire extinguisher and dust went everywhere on the floor, clothes, and it was difficult for the employees to breath. For the safety of the employees and customers, we may not open until an hour or two later. People kept coming to the door of the store and the manager kept saying the same thing over and over until we finally opened at 11 am. I worked from 10 am to 3 pm and by the end of the shift, my feet were killing me even with the two 15 minute breaks.

The food court was 10 minutes away so by the time you got your food; it was time to be back on your post. I learned to bring my lunch plus it was expensive to eat in the Mall. That day was also my granddaughters' birthday and my oldest daughter was giving her a birthday celebration at home. I got off and headed home to get some rest before the party. I was at home for about 1 hour when I got a call from my manager asking if I would be interested in working an overnight shift from 10p to 7a.

I explained to him that it was my granddaughters' birthday and I could work the shift but it would have to be 11p. He said that would be fine and he let me know that it was a $1 more night differential. I was happy about that. After I hung up the phone with the manager, I got a frantic call from my oldest daughter; she was on her way to the store with the kids when she got a flat tire. Omg, she was panting and out of breath and her husband was at work. She asked me to pick her and the kids up and take them to the store to grab some pizza.

I grabbed my youngest daughter, got halfway dressed and headed to pick her and the kids up. It took me about 20 minutes to get to them but they were so happy to see us. I had about 2 hours before I had to be at work, so I enjoyed the birthday celebration and put on the rest of my uniform and headed to work.

When I arrived at the Mall, all the managers were leaving. So there was a crew of about eight people who were cleaning the shelves, floors and restocking all the items. I spoke with the crew manager and he said he got the call out of the blue to come and clean the store and that this was his first contract with the store. So I babysitted the workers until 7 am. It was so hot in the stock room so I texted the manager and asked if I could take off my jacket and remove my tie, he replied "absolutely." The night ran pretty smoothly with no incidents. I was off the following day, so I was able to rest.

The next time I had to go to work was during the week. The manager had given me a schedule; he mentioned that I could get about 35 hours this week because there was a big after-Christmas sale. I worked the first day with no incident, but I noticed the politics that went on in the store. The customers were allowed to bring in packages from other stores, walk all around the store with them and even take them to the fitting room.

Some stores will need you to check your bags at the counter but not this store. Each item had sensors on them but customers could pop those sensors off and load their bags and walk right out the front door. That was just the beginning, customers had bags and items that other stores left the sensors on and it would buzz every time that happened. If the cashiers left a sensor or forgot to deactivate shoes or purses, the buzzer would go off. That was very stressful because you have to get to the door once you hear the buzzer. I think I heard that buzzer in my sleep!

I made it through my 2nd day but on my 3rd day, 15 minutes before it was time to go, I was doing my rounds and I spotted a bag on the floor stuffed from another store. I was about to pick it up when a customer ran over and said "oh I was looking for this," I said, "are you sure it's your bag"? He immediately got very defensive and loud in the store. I took offense and got loud with him and ordered him out of the store. We started arguing and he told me I better get out of his face and I said: "what are you going to do"?

So instead of me de-escalating the issue, I took it to level 10! I signed out and had a manager sign my timecard; I went to the car, took off my jacket and tie. I went back to the store, but the person was gone and I was still furious. I asked an associate to purchase a bag for me with his discount and I gave him cash to purchase it for me. I had to wait until he got off to get the bag. While I was waiting, I texted the manager and I let him know that this position was not a good fit and that my last day was that day.

I had to apologize for the short notice but I could not handle disrespect from the customers, managers, and the staff. While the customer was threatening me, the managers and staff were standing there like it was ok. This was how the store operated and I did not want to be a part of this madness. I found out so much about that mall and I am so glad I do not have to go back there again. Somehow, I missed the memo about this mall. I did meet a cool girl and we became friends fast. She had my back about how the managers did not take our side. I sent the manager a text asking when I would be paid but you know I didn't get a response.

I found another security job part-time and I still have a few decisions to make.

I am contemplating divorce for the 4th time and I am praying for a peaceful decision. I added legal to my benefits last year and I am getting an attorney and consultation any day now. I have been stalked, talked about, and lied on but that's ok because I am free! I want my last name back, the name I was born with, my family name "Mays." When I think of His goodness and all that I have been through, I thank God that I don't look like what I've been through. I have a shine from God above and a joy that keeps me. Pray for my family and me.

ABOUT THE AUTHOR

I graduated from Gwinnett Technical College with my ATT degree as a Microcomputer Specialist in 2005. I am working on my BAS in Administrative Management at Clayton State and I will be graduating in December 2018! I Have three children, Glenn Sims, Donesha Wells and Sanaa Griffin. I have four grandchildren, Jaiden, Trinity, Makenzie, and King. I am surrounded by love and I enjoy being with my family. I work full-time and part-time. I have been at my current job for 17 years. I plan on getting my Master's Degree in Human Services. I am the Founder and Executive Director of Girls Empowered Mentored and Supported which I began in January 2016 (www.thegemsinc.org). I enjoy gospel music, writing and going to church.

Interested in Writing and/or Publishing a

Book???

Visit www.A2ZBookspublishing.net

CPSIA information can be obtained
at www.ICGtesting.com
Printed in the USA
FSHW010537011118
53447FS